CW00400115

Paleo |
for Beginners

*Nourishing Grain-Free Recipes for a
Healthy Lifestyle*

Aliza King

© Copyright 2021 by - Aliza King - All rights reserved.

The following Book is reproduced below with the goal of providing information that is as accurate and reliable as possible. Regardless, purchasing this Book can be seen as consent to the fact that both the publisher and the author of this book are in no way experts on the topics discussed within and that any recommendations or suggestions that are made herein are for entertainment purposes only. Professionals should be consulted as needed prior to undertaking any of the action endorsed herein.

This declaration is deemed fair and valid by both the American Bar Association and the Committee of Publishers Association and is legally binding throughout the United States.

Furthermore, the transmission, duplication, or reproduction of any of the following work including specific information will be considered an illegal act irrespective of if it is done electronically or in print. This extends to creating a secondary or tertiary copy of the work or a recorded copy and is only allowed with the express written consent from the Publisher. All additional right reserved.

The information in the following pages is broadly considered a truthful and accurate account of facts and as such, any inattention, use, or misuse of the information in question by the reader will render any resulting actions solely under their purview. There are no scenarios in which the publisher or the original author of this work can be in any fashion deemed liable for any hardship or damages that may befall them after undertaking information described herein.

Additionally, the information in the following pages is intended only for informational purposes and should thus be thought of as universal. As befitting its nature, it is presented without assurance regarding its prolonged validity or interim quality. Trademarks that are mentioned are done without written consent and can in no way be considered an endorsement from the trademark holder.

TABLE OF CONTENTS

Introduction

The Paleo Diet is a modern plan to replicate the diet of the humans that lived during the Paleolithic period. Our ancestors hunted and gathered their food consisting primarily of animal protein and plants. They used to eat foods that our bodies were designed for, lean meat and fish, eggs, fruits and vegetables, nuts and seeds, and healthy fats.

Modern technology has provided other forms of food available to us, grains, dairy, processed foods, sugars, and trans fats that are not as adaptable for our bodies to digest properly. The Paleo Diet provides our bodies with more efficient energy that helps to aid us in burning fat, with the benefit of weight loss.

The Paleo Diet is the best way to lose weight as improve your health.

This way of eating is even good for people who suffer from insomnia and mood swings, depressions, or anxieties. If you have skin problems, the Paleo Diet helps cleaning your body internally, fight acne, and maintain the gut flora.

Other benefits of the Paleo Diet are:

- Allergy reducing
- Increasing of energy level

- Relieving asthma symptoms
- Improving immune functions and lipid profile (the Paleo diet is one of the types of Anti-Inflammatory Diet)
- Blood sugar regulation

It also provides clearer skin, and teeth health. This diet aids with the prevention or control of many modern diseases today such as diabetes, and cardiovascular diseases.

PALEO RECIPES

AVOCADO BURGER WITH SALMON

Time required:
30 minutes

Servings: 01

INGREDIENTS

1 Avocado
2 slices of smoked salmon
Sesame seeds

STEPS FOR COOKING

1. Cut the avocado in half, peel it and remove the core.
2. Place the smoked salmon in between the two an avocado part.
3. Add some sesame seeds.

Vanilla Pancakes

Time required:
25 minutes

Servings: 06

INGREDIENTS

½ cup of coconut milk

2 eggs, beaten

1 teaspoon vanilla extract

1 teaspoon baking powder

1 teaspoon lemon juice

1 cup almond flour

1 tablespoon raw honey

STEPS FOR COOKING

1. In the big bowl mix up coconut milk and eggs.

2. Add vanilla extract, baking powder, and lemon juicer.

3. When the liquid is homogenous, add the almond flour.

4. Stir the mixture with the help of the hand whisker until it is homogenous and without lumps.

5. Preheat the non-stick skillet well.

6. Then pour the pancake batter into the hot skillet with the help of the ladle (1 ladle = 1 pancake).

7. Cook the pancake for 1 minute and flip it on another side. Cook it for 30 seconds more or until the pancake is light brown.

INGREDIENTS

STEPS FOR COOKING

8. Repeat the same steps with all remaining batter.

9. Sprinkle the cooker pancakes with honey.

PALEO BREAKFAST EGG MUFFINS

Time required:
25 minutes

Servings: 08

INGREDIENTS

8 eggs

1 cup of diced broccoli

1 cup of diced mushrooms

1 cup of diced onion

Salt and pepper

STEPS FOR COOKING

1. Preheat your oven to 350 degrees.

2. Dice all your vegetables. You can add more or less of any of them, but keep the overall portion of vegetables the same for the best results.

3. In your large-sized mixing bowl, whisk together your eggs, vegetables, pepper, and salt.

4. Pour your mixture into your greased muffin pan, the mixture should evenly fill about 8 muffin cups.

5. Bake approximately 18 to 20 minutes, or until your toothpick inserted in the middle comes out clean.

6. Serve and Enjoy!

Spiced Orange Breakfast Couscous

Time required:
20 minutes

Servings: 04

INGREDIENTS

3 cups orange juice

1.1/2 cups couscous

1 teaspoon ground cinnamon

1/4 teaspoon ground cloves

1/2 cup dried fruit

1/2 cup chopped almonds

STEPS FOR COOKING

1. Take the orange juice to a boil. Add the couscous, cinnamon, and cloves and remove from heat. Shield the pan and allow sitting until the couscous softens.

2. Fluff the couscous and stir in the dried fruit and nuts. Serve - immediately. Pecans and syrup. Serve hot.

HAM AND ZUCCHINI FRITTATA

Time required:
30 minutes

Servings: 06

INGREDIENTS

1 1/4 cups diced ham

1 cup grated zucchini (pat dry)

1 cup diced green bell pepper

One medium onion diced

12 eggs whisked

1 1/2 tablespoons minced

Italian parsley

1 1/2 tablespoons coconut oil

STEPS FOR COOKING

1. In an ovenproof skillet, heat the oil over medium heat, and add in the peppers and onion. Sauté. Add in the ham, and zucchini, and sauté for 5 min. Add in the parsley.

2. Spread the vegetable and ham mixture evenly on the bottom of the skillet. Pour in the whisked egg over the top of the mixture.

3. Cook on medium-low for 5 min, until the edges cook.

4. Place the pan into a preheated oven at 350°, and cook for 15 min until the frittata is firm in the middle when the pan is shaken.

Eggs Benedict with Hollandaise Sauce

Time required:
35 minutes

Servings: 02

INGREDIENTS

2 potato toasts

2 eggs

2 bacon slices

Apple vinegar

Green onion

Coconut oil

1 cup of water

2 yolks

1 Tbsp. of lemon juice

Salt and Pepper

1/2 cup of ghee

STEPS FOR COOKING

1. Mix the yolks, the water, and the lemon juice together in a bowl. Set the bowl in a pan filled with some boiling water.

2. Place the pan on the heat and beat the yolks until you obtain a thick and frothy compound. Add salt pepper and the ghee and keep on beating for about 5 minutes.

3. Cook the bacon and prepare the poached eggs.

4. Serve the dish placing the potato toast with one bacon slice and the egg on top of it. Add 2 spoons of sauce.

PALEO GRANOLA

Time required:
28 minutes

Servings: 04

INGREDIENTS

½ cup almonds

2 oz cashew

3 oz pumpkin seeds

½ cup coconut flakes

1 tablespoon raw honey

1 tablespoon poppy seeds

1 teaspoon vanilla extract

½ teaspoon ground cardamom

1 tablespoon coconut oil

STEPS FOR COOKING

1. Put the almonds, cashew, pumpkin seeds, and coconut flakes in the blender.

2. Blend the mixture for 5 seconds.

3. Transfer it to the bowl.

4. Add raw honey, poppy seeds, vanilla extract, ground cardamom, and coconut oil.

5. Stir the mixture until homogenous.

6. Line the baking tray with baking paper.

7. Put the granola mixture on the tray and flatten it.

8. Preheat the oven to 350F.

9. Put the tray with granola in the oven and cook it for 10-15 minutes or until

INGREDIENTS	STEPS FOR COOKING
	it is dry, then crack the granola into the pieces. 10. Store it in the dry closed jar.

Paleo Shrimp and Grits

Time required:
45 minutes

Servings: 04

INGREDIENTS

Shrimp:

15 pieces of raw shrimp, shelled and deveined

3 tablespoons of extra-virgin olive oil

6 cloves of minced garlic

1 lemon, zested

2 teaspoons of dried oregano

2 slices of bacon

1/2 large diced onion

2 tablespoons of butter

1 tablespoon of white wine vinegar

STEPS FOR COOKING

1. In your medium-sized bowl mix together your olive oil, lemon zest, 2 cloves of garlic, and 1 teaspoon of dried oregano. Place your shrimp in your bowl and marinate for approximately 1 to 3 hours.

2. Place a couple of inches of water in your large-sized pot. Once your water is boiling, place steamer insert and then cauliflower florets into your pot and cover. Steam for approximately 12 to 14 minutes, until completely tender. Drain and return your cauliflower to the pot.

3. Add your milk, garlic, and ghee to the cauliflower. Using an immersion blender, combine your ingredients. The cauliflower should be fairly thick

INGREDIENTS

1 teaspoon of Red Pepper Flakes

1 tablespoon of lemon juice

1 tablespoon of chopped fresh oregano

Salt and freshly ground black pepper

Grits:

1 large head of cauliflower, cut into florets

1/4 cup of almond milk

4 cloves of minced garlic

1 tablespoon of ghee

1/4 teaspoon of cayenne pepper

Pepper and Salt

STEPS FOR COOKING

to resemble the consistency of grits. Season with pepper and salt.

4. Cook your bacon in a large-sized skillet over medium heat until crispy. Reserving the bacon fat in your pan, set your bacon to the side to cool and break into pieces.

5. Add your butter to the bacon fat in the pan and allow it to melt. Add your onion and sauté for approximately 4 to 5 minutes until softened. Add in your remaining 4 garlic cloves, red pepper flakes, and dried oregano. Sauté for about 1 to 2 minutes, stirring frequently.

6. Stir in your white wine vinegar, and then add your shrimp. Cook, stirring frequently until your shrimp are cooked through, approximately 3 to 4 minutes. Remove from heat and stir in your lemon juice. Season with pepper and salt. Place your shrimp and onions over grits, with bacon and fresh oregano as your garnish.

7. Serve and Enjoy!

SAVORY OATMEAL PORRIDGE

Time required:
25 minutes

Servings: 04

INGREDIENTS

2 1/2 cups vegetable broth

2 1/2 cups milk

1/2 cup steel-cut oats

1 tablespoon faro

1/2 cup slivered almonds

1/4 cup Nutritional yeast

2 cups old-fashioned rolled oats

1/2 teaspoon salt (optional)

STEPS FOR COOKING

1. Take the broth and almond milk to a boil. Add the oats, faro, almond slivers, and Nutritional yeast.

2. Cook over medium-high heat for about 20 minutes, then stir occasionally.

3. Add the rolled oats and cook for another 5 minutes, until creamy. Stir in the salt (if using).

4. Divide into four single-serving containers. Let cool before sealing the lids.

COCONUT CREPES

Time required:
20 minutes

Servings: 06

INGREDIENTS

1 cup coconut flour

2 tablespoons coconut flakes

1 teaspoon vanilla extract

3 eggs, beaten

¼ cup Erythritol

¼ teaspoon ground cardamom

½ teaspoon baking soda

1 teaspoon apple cider vinegar

1/3 cup coconut milk

STEPS FOR COOKING

1. Put all ingredients from the list above in the big bowl and mix up until you get the smooth batter.

2. After this, preheat the non-sticky skillet well.

3. Pour the crepe batter into the preheated skillet with the help of the ladle and flatten the batter in the shape of the crepe.

4. Cook it for 1 minute.

5. Carefully flip the crepe on another side and cook it for 30 seconds more.

6. Repeat the same steps with the remaining batter.

FRENCH TOASTS

Time required:
25 minutes

Servings: 04

INGREDIENTS

4 slices of Paleo
banana bread

2 eggs, beaten

2 tablespoons
coconut cream

1 tablespoon
Erythritol

1 teaspoon vanilla
extract

½ teaspoon ground
cinnamon

1 tablespoon
coconut oil

STEPS FOR COOKING

1. In the mixing bowl mix up eggs, coconut cream, Erythritol, vanilla extract, and ground cinnamon.

2. Then coat the banana bread slices in the egg mixture from each side.

3. Toss the coconut oil in the skillet and melt it.

4. Put the coated banana bread slices in the melted oil in one layer and cook them for 2 minutes from each side over medium-high heat.

5. The cooked toasts will have a golden brown color.

PEANUT BUTTER BITES

Time required:
10 minutes

Servings: 05

INGREDIENTS

1 cup rolled oats

12 Medjool dates, pitted

½ cup peanut butter, sugar-free

STEPS FOR COOKING

1. Plug in a blender or a food processor, add all the ingredients in its jar, and then cover with the lid.

2. Pulse for 5 minutes until well combined, and then tip the mixture into a shallow dish.

3. Shape the mixture into 20 balls, 1 tablespoon of mixture per ball, and then serve.

Turkey Breakfast Sandwich

Time required:
10 minutes

Servings: 01

INGREDIENTS

2 oz. turkey meat, roasted and thinly sliced

2 tbsp. pecans, toasted and chopped

2 oz. Brie cheese, sliced

2 slices sourdough bread

2 tbsp. cranberry chutney

¼ cup arugula

STEPS FOR COOKING

1. In a bowl, mix pecans with chutney and stir well.
2. Spread this on a bread slice, add turkey slices, brie cheese, and arugula, and top with the other bread slice.
3. Serve right away.
4. Enjoy!

CRUNCHY GREEN BANANAS STICKS

Time required:
15 minutes

Servings: 02

INGREDIENTS

2 green bananas
3 Tbsp. of nuts
3 Tbsp. of almonds
1 Tbsp. of coconut
sugar
1/2 tsp. of cinnamon
2 Tbsp. of coconut
oil

STEPS FOR COOKING

1. Mix the nuts and the almonds in a mixer. In a bowl, mix the compound together with the coconut sugar and cinnamon.

2. Peel and cut the bananas into strips.

3. Dip the strips into the nuts and almonds mixture.

4. Preheat a pan over medium heat with some coconut oil; cook 3-4 strips by time until golden.

Coconut Truffles

Time required:
20 minutes

Servings: 14

INGREDIENTS

1 cup of grated coconut

4 Tbsp. of almonds

4 Tbsp. of cashews

4 Tbsp. of walnuts

1 Tbsp. of honey

1/4 tsp. of vanilla powder

1 Tbsp. of coconut milk

3 Tbsp. of coconut oil

14 almonds

Grated coconut for decoration

STEPS FOR COOKING

1. In a mixer mix the almonds, the cashews, the walnuts, and the grated coconut. (Keep 14 almonds for the filling).

2. Add the coconut oil, the honey, the vanilla powder, and the coconut milk and mix again.

3. Shape 15 grams balls, and fill each of them with 1 almond.

4. Roll them into the grated coconut and refrigerate for 1 hour.

TOMATO MEATBALLS

Time required:
45 minutes

Servings: 05

INGREDIENTS

1 cup ground chicken

10 oz ground pork

½ zucchini, grated

1 teaspoon chili flakes

1 teaspoon Italian seasonings

½ teaspoon ground black pepper

1 teaspoon ground nutmeg

1 tablespoon tapioca flour

½ cup crushed tomatoes

1 teaspoon coconut cream

STEPS FOR COOKING

1. Make the meatballs: in the mixing bowl mix up ground chicken, grated zucchini, ground pork, chili flakes, and Italian seasonings.

2. Then add ground black pepper and ground nutmeg. Mix up the meat mixture until it is smooth and make the small meatballs.

3. After this, grease the baking tray with coconut oil and put the meatballs in one layer.

4. Preheat the oven to 365F.

5. Put the tray with meatballs in the oven and bake them for 10 minutes.

6. Meanwhile, make the tomato sauce: in the mixing bowl mix up tapioca flour, crushed tomatoes, and coconut cream.

INGREDIENTS	STEPS FOR COOKING
1 teaspoon coconut oil	7. Blend the mixture with the help of the immersion blender until it is smooth and pour in the saucepan. 8. Bring the tomato sauce to boil. 9. After this, pour the sauce over the meatballs and bake the meal for 15 minutes more.

LEMON CHICKEN THIGHS

Time required:
55 minutes

Servings: 04

INGREDIENTS

8 chicken thighs, skinless, boneless

½ lemon, sliced

1 teaspoon ground black pepper

1 tablespoon coconut oil

1 teaspoon dried parsley

½ teaspoon salt

1 teaspoon chili flakes

½ teaspoon garlic powder

¼ cup of coconut milk

STEPS FOR COOKING

1. In the mixing bowl mix up garlic powder, chili flakes, salt, dried parsley, and ground black pepper.

2. Then rub the chicken thighs with the spice mixture and leave for 10 minutes to marinate.

3. After this, grease the baking pan with coconut oil.

4. Put the chicken thighs in the prepared baking pan and top with the sliced lemon and coconut milk.

5. Preheat the oven to 365F.

6. Put the baking pan with chicken in the preheated oven and cook for 40 minutes.

MUSHROOMS AND CHARD SOUP

Time required:
40 minutes

Servings: 04

INGREDIENTS	STEPS FOR COOKING

INGREDIENTS

3 cups Swiss chard, chopped

6 cups vegetable stock

1 cup mushrooms, sliced

2 garlic cloves, minced

1 tablespoon olive oil

2 scallions, chopped

2 tablespoons balsamic vinegar

1/4 cup basil, chopped

Salt and black pepper to the taste

1 tablespoon chopped cilantro

STEPS FOR COOKING

1. Heat up the oil in a pot placed over medium-high heat; add the scallions and the garlic and sauté for 5 minutes.

2. Add the mushrooms, then sauté for another 5 minutes.

3. Add the rest of the ingredients, toss, bring to a simmer, then cook over medium heat for 20 minutes more.

4. Ladle the soup into bowls and serve.

GREEN PEA SOUP

Time required:
55 minutes

Servings: 06

INGREDIENTS

*1 (16-ounce)
package dried green
split peas, soaked
overnight*

*5 cups vegetable
broth or water*

*2 teaspoons garlic
powder*

*2 teaspoons onion
powder*

*1 teaspoon dried
oregano*

*1 teaspoon dried
thyme*

*¼ teaspoon freshly
ground black pepper*

STEPS FOR COOKING

1. Combine the split peas, broth, garlic powder, onion powder, oregano, thyme, and pepper in a stockpot.
2. Bring to a boil over medium-high heat.
3. Cover, lower the heat to medium-low and allow to simmer for 45 minutes, stirring every 5 to 10 minutes.
4. Serve warm.

CHANTERELLE GRATIN

Time required:
30 minutes

Servings: 04

INGREDIENTS

2 shallots

400 g chanterelles

200 g young, tender nettle leaves

200 g young spinach leaves

100 g cream salt and pepper

freshly grated nutmeg

80 g grated parmesan cheese

2 cloves of garlic

2 tbsp. butter

100 ml milk

2 eggs

STEPS FOR COOKING

1. Set the oven to 200 C. Remove the shell and chop the shallots and garlic. Clean the mushrooms, just rub them with a brush or with damp kitchen paper.

2. Place the nettles on the worktop (use disposable gloves), roll with the rolling pin. In this way, the nettles will be broken and will not cause pain. Remove all stems. Clean and dry the nettles and spinach, then chop.

3. Dissolve a tablespoon of butter. Steam the shallots without letting them turn color. Add the garlic and let the mushrooms follow too. Sauté everything for about three to four minutes while stirring then mix in the nettles and spinach, pepper.

INGREDIENTS	STEPS FOR COOKING
	4. Set a casserole dish with butter and pour the contents of the pan into it. Bring the cream and milk to temperature in a saucepan, mix in the eggs, season with a little salt, pepper, and nutmeg to taste. Spread the sauce over the mushroom mixture, sprinkle with a little Parmesan and bake in the oven on the middle rack for about a quarter of an hour until the surface has a crust.

WOK VEGETABLES WITH TOFU

Time required:
25 minutes

Servings: 04

INGREDIENTS

1 organic lemon

8 stalks of mint

3 centimeters of fresh ginger

1 red chili pepper

4 tbsp. neutral oil

Salt

400 g broad green beans

2 red peppers

2 spring onions

400 g tofu

150 ml vegetable stock, instant

STEPS FOR COOKING

1. Wash and dry the lemon, rub the peel. Clean and dry the mint and remove the leaves. Remove the peel from the ginger and cut. Clean the chili pepper, remove the seeds. Finely chop the mint, ginger, and chili. Mix with the zest of the lemon, a tablespoon of oil, and salt.

2. Clean the beans and remove the end pieces, cut the beans diagonally into pieces just under one centimeter wide. Boil enough water in a saucepan, season with salt, and boil the beans for about two minutes. Pour into a sieve, pour cold water over it and allow draining. Clean the peppers, cut them into quarters, and remove the seeds and the walls. Cut the quarters of the peppers into

INGREDIENTS	STEPS FOR COOKING
	strips. Set and wash the spring onions and cut them into rings. Drain the tofu and dice it an inch.
	3. Bring the wok to temperature and add oil. Add the tofu, season with salt, and fry for about four minutes until crispy. Add the vegetables and onions and stir-fry for about three minutes. Fry the herb paste, add the stock, and season with salt. Serve the vegetables immediately. Rice or Asian noodles go well with it.

CHICKEN AND EGG SALAD

Time required:
15 minutes

Servings: 06

INGREDIENTS

2 cups cooked chicken, chopped

2 hard-boiled eggs, diced

2-3 pickled gherkins, chopped

1 large apple, diced

1/2 cup walnuts, baked

4 tbsp lemon juice

2 tbsp olive oil

salt and pepper, to taste

STEPS FOR COOKING

1. Bake walnuts in a single layer in a preheated to 480 F oven for 3 minutes or until toasted and fragrant, stirring halfway through.

2. Stir together chicken, apple, eggs, and gherkins. Combine lemon juice, olive oil, salt, and pepper to taste and add to the chicken mixture.

3. Sprinkle with walnuts and serve.

GREEN LETTUCE AND TUNA SALAD

Time required:
15 minutes

Servings: 04

INGREDIENTS

1 head green lettuce, washed and drained

1 cucumber, cut

1 can tuna, drained and broken into big chunks

a bunch of radishes, cut

a bunch of spring onions, finely cut

juice of a half lemon or 2 tbsp of white wine vinegar

3 tbsp olive oil

salt to taste

STEPS FOR COOKING

1. Cut the lettuce into thin strips. Slice the cucumber and the radishes as thinly as possible, then chop the spring onions.

2. Mix all the vegetables in a large bowl, add the tuna, and season with lemon juice, oil, and salt to taste.

Rainbow Vegetables with Chicken Meatballs

Time required:
65 minutes

Servings: 04

INGREDIENTS

1 sweet red pepper, sliced

1 zucchini, sliced

2 tomatoes, sliced

1 eggplant, sliced

2 cups ground chicken

1 egg, beaten

1 teaspoon ground black pepper

1 teaspoon chili flakes

1 teaspoon coconut oil

STEPS FOR COOKING

1. In the mixing bowl mix up ground chicken, egg, ground black pepper, dried cilantro, thyme, and salt.

2. Then make the small meatballs from the chicken mixture.

3. Grease the baking pan with coconut oil.

4. Put the zucchini, sweet red pepper, tomatoes, and eggplant in the greased baking pan one by one.

5. Put the chicken meatballs in the center of the vegetable mixture.

6. Then sprinkle the meal with sunflower oil and chili flakes.

7. Preheat the oven to 365F.

INGREDIENTS

1 teaspoon dried cilantro

1 teaspoon dried thyme

1 teaspoon sunflower oil

1 teaspoon salt

STEPS FOR COOKING

8. Put the baking pan with the meal in the oven and cook it for 45 minutes.

Lettuce Wraps with Prosciutto

Time required:
20 minutes

Servings: 04

INGREDIENTS

1 cup lettuce leaves

5 oz prosciutto, sliced

2 tomatoes, sliced

1 cucumber, sliced

4 teaspoons coconut cream

STEPS FOR COOKING

1. Separate the lettuce leaves into 4 parts.

2. Then place all lettuce leaves on the chopping board or any smooth surface overlap. In the end, you should get 4 lettuce "blankets".

3. Put the tomatoes, cucumber, and prosciutto on the lettuce.

4. Then sprinkle the mixture with coconut cream and roll into the wraps.

5. Secure the lettuce wraps with toothpicks if needed.

Scallion and Mint Soup

Time required:
20 minutes

Servings: 04

INGREDIENTS

6 cups vegetable broth

¼ cup fresh mint leaves, roughly chopped

¼ cup chopped scallions

3 garlic cloves, minced

3 tablespoons freshly squeezed lime juice

STEPS FOR COOKING

1. In a large stockpot, combine the broth, mint, scallions, garlic, and lime juice, then bring to a boil over medium-high heat.

2. Cover, reduce the heat to low, simmer for 15 minutes, and serve.

HERBAL FRITTATA WITH PEPPERS AND FETA

Time required:
25 minutes

Servings: 04

INGREDIENTS

5 eggs

Sea-salt

1 bunch of parsley

4 tbsp. freshly
grated parmesan

2 red peppers

1 yellow pepper

150 g feta

3 tbsp. olive oil

Salt and pepper

STEPS FOR COOKING

1. Mix the eggs in a bowl with a pinch of sea salt. Clean and dry the parsley, peel off the leaves, and chop. Stir the parsley and parmesan into the eggs. Divide the peppers lengthways, clean, wash and cut into strips. Crumble the feta.

2. Bring the olive oil to temperature in a pan. Add the paprika strips and steam for about two minutes, season with a little salt and pepper.

3. Stream the egg mixture over it and spread the feta on top. Cover and let the frittata stand for six to eight minutes over moderate heat.

4. Slide on a platter, cut into pieces and serve warm or cold.

Paleo Roasted Carrots

Time required:
55 minutes

Servings: 04

INGREDIENTS

1 and 1/2 pounds young carrots (yellow, purple, and red ones)

2 tbsp. balsamic vinegar

2 garlic cloves, finely minced

2 tbsp. ghee

1 tbsp. honey

Salt and black pepper to taste

A handful of parsley leaves, finely chopped

STEPS FOR COOKING

1. In a bowl, mix vinegar with ghee, honey, garlic, salt, and pepper to the taste and stir very well.
2. Add carrots and toss to coat.
3. Transfer this to a baking dish, introduce it to the oven at 400 degrees and bake for 30 minutes.
4. Take carrots out of the oven, sprinkle parsley on top, toss gently, and serve right away as a side dish.
5. Enjoy!

MEDITERRANEAN BEEF SALAD

Time required:
15 minutes

Servings: 02

INGREDIENTS

8 oz roast beef, thinly sliced

6 cups assorted greens, torn

2 carrots, grated

6-7 fresh mushrooms, thinly sliced

4 tbsp fresh basil leaves, torn

Ba 2 tbsp lemon juice

4 tbsp olive oil

1 tsp salt

STEPS FOR COOKING

1. Prepare the dressing by mixing lemon juice, olive oil, crushed garlic, salt, and basil leaves in a bowl.

2. Divide greens among four plates. Arrange beef with vegetables and mushrooms on top. Drizzle with dressing.

RED ONION SKEWERS

Time required:
30 minutes

Servings: 02

INGREDIENTS

2 red onions, peeled

1 tablespoon olive oil

1 teaspoon lemon juice

¼ teaspoon salt

STEPS FOR COOKING

1. Chop the red onion roughly and separate it into the petals.
2. Then string the red onion petals in the skewers and sprinkle with lemon juice, salt, and olive oil.
3. Preheat the oven to 365F.
4. Put the onion skewers in the tray and transfer them to the oven.
5. Bake the onion skewers for 15 minutes or until the onion is light brown.

Pancetta Wrapped Asparagus

Time required:
35 minutes

Servings: 08

INGREDIENTS

7 oz pancetta, sliced
1-pound asparagus
½ teaspoon salt
1 teaspoon olive oil

STEPS FOR COOKING

1. Preheat the oven to 365F.
2. Line the baking tray with baking paper.
3. After cut the asparagus and wrap eat in the pancetta.
4. Place the wrapped asparagus in the tray and sprinkle with olive oil and salt.
5. Bake the asparagus for 25 minutes or until the pancetta is cooked.

BASIL CHICKEN WINGS

Time required:
40 minutes

Servings: 04

INGREDIENTS

1-pound chicken wings, boneless

1 tablespoon dried basil

1 teaspoon salt

1 tablespoon sesame oil

STEPS FOR COOKING

1. Sprinkle the chicken wings with dried basil, salt, and sesame oil.
2. Then arrange them in the baking tray.
3. Preheat the oven to 365F.
4. Put the tray with the chicken wings in the oven and cook for 30 minutes or until the wings are golden brown.

MANGO MEATBALLS

Time required:
30 minutes

Servings: 04

INGREDIENTS

1 tablespoon mango puree

1 cup ground chicken

½ cup ground beef

1 teaspoon dried oregano

1 tablespoon almond flour

1 teaspoon olive oil

1 tablespoon flax meal

½ teaspoon chili flakes

STEPS FOR COOKING

1. In the mixing bowl, mix up mango puree, ground chicken, ground beef, oregano, almond flour, flax meal, and chili flakes.

2. Make the small meatballs.

3. After this, pour the olive oil into the skillet and heat it up.

4. Add the meatballs to the skillet and cook them for 4 minutes from each side.

LAMB STEW

Time required:
3 hours 10
minutes

———————

Servings: 02

INGREDIENTS

*1/2 lb. lamb,
boneless*

*1/4 cup green olives,
sliced*

*2 tablespoon lemon
juice*

1/2 onion, chopped

*2 garlic cloves,
minced*

2 fresh thyme sprigs

*1/4 teaspoon
turmeric*

1/2 teaspoon pepper

1/4 teaspoon salt

*1/2 teaspoon
sesame seeds*

STEPS FOR COOKING

1. Slice the lamb into thin pieces.
2. Add every ingredient into a pot and stir.
3. Cover and cook on low flame for 3 hours.
4. Stir well, garnish with sesame seeds and serve.

PREMIUM ROASTED BABY POTATOES

Time required:
45 minutes

Servings: 04

INGREDIENTS

2 pounds new yellow potatoes, scrubbed and cut into wedges

2 tablespoons extra virgin olive oil

2 teaspoons fresh rosemary, chopped

1 teaspoon garlic powder

1 teaspoon sweet paprika

½ teaspoon sea salt

½ teaspoon freshly ground black pepper

STEPS FOR COOKING

1. Preheat your oven to 400 degrees Fahrenheit.

2. Take a large bowl and add potatoes, olive oil, garlic, rosemary, paprika, sea salt, and pepper.

3. Spread potatoes in a single layer on a baking sheet, then bake for 35 minutes.

4. Serve and enjoy!

Yogurt Chicken and Red Onion Mix

Time required:
40 minutes

Servings: 04

INGREDIENTS

2 pounds chicken breast (skinless, boneless, sliced)

3 tablespoons olive oil

¼ cup Greek yogurt

2 garlic cloves, minced

½ teaspoon onion powder

A pinch of salt and black pepper

4 red onions, sliced

STEPS FOR COOKING

1. In a roasting pan, combine the chicken with the oil, the yogurt, and the other ingredients, introduce it in the oven at 375 degrees F and bake for 30 minutes.

2. Divide the chicken mix between plates and serve hot.

PALEO GLAZED SALMON

Time required:
35 minutes

Servings: 04

INGREDIENTS

2 tbsp. pure maple syrup

4 salmon fillets, skin-on

Salt and white pepper to taste

2 tsp. Dijon mustard

Juice and zest from 1 orange

2 garlic cloves, finely chopped

STEPS FOR COOKING

1. In a bowl, mix maple syrup with orange zest, juice, mustard, salt, pepper, and garlic, and whisk well.

2. Arrange salmon in a baking dish, brush with the maple syrup and orange mix, set in the oven at 400 F, and bake.

3. Divide between plates and serve right away.

4. Enjoy!

PALEO GRILLED CALAMARI

Time required:
35 minutes

Servings: 04

INGREDIENTS

2 lb. calamari,
tentacles, and tubes
sliced into rings

1 lime, sliced

lemon, sliced

1 orange, sliced

2 tbsp. parsley,
chopped

Salt and black
pepper to taste

3 tbsp. lemon juice

1/4 cup extra virgin
olive oil

2 garlic cloves,
minced

STEPS FOR COOKING

1. In a bowl, mix calamari with sliced lemon, lime, orange, lemon juice, salt, pepper, parsley, garlic, and olive oil and toss to coat.

2. Heat up your kitchen grill over medium-high heat, add calamari and fruit slices, cook for 5 minutes, divide between plates and serve.

3. Enjoy!

Broccoli Bacon Frittata

Time required:
20 minutes

Servings: 04

INGREDIENTS

2 tbsp canned coconut milk

1 cup broccoli florets

3 spring onions, finely chopped

3 strips bacon, cooked and crumbled

1 large tomato, sliced

2 tbsp olive oil

Salt and black pepper to taste

STEPS FOR COOKING

1. Steam broccoli florets until soft. Beat eggs, coconut milk, salt, and pepper.

2. Heat olive oil in a medium baking dish. Add broccoli and bacon and stir. Cook for 1 minute.

3. Pour over the egg mixture and stir again. Add in spring onions.

4. Cover with sliced tomato and bake in a preheated to 350 F oven for 15 minutes.

Swordfish Kebabs

Time required:
25 minutes

Servings: 04

INGREDIENTS

2 zucchinis, cut into
2-inch cubes

2 lbs skinless
swordfish steaks, cut
into 2-inch cubes

1 cup cherry
tomatoes

1/2 cup basil leaves,
finely chopped

4 garlic cloves,
crushed

1 lemon, juiced rind
from 1 lemon

olive oil cooking
spray

STEPS FOR COOKING

1. Prepare marinade by combining garlic,
   lemon rind, lemon juice, basil leaves,
   salt, and pepper in a small bowl.

2. Thread fish cubes onto skewers, then
   zucchinis and tomatoes.

3. Place skewers in a shallow plate.
   Brush with marinade and refrigerate
   for 30 minutes if time permits.

4. Spray skewers with olive oil spray and
   bake on a preheated barbecue plate
   on medium heat.

5. Bake for 6-7 minutes, turning, or until
   fish is just cooked through.

BANANA MUFFINS WITH CARDAMOM

Time required:
20 minutes

Servings: 06

INGREDIENTS

4 eggs, beaten

1 teaspoon ground cardamom

1 teaspoon baking powder

4 tablespoons coconut cream

3 bananas, mashed

4 tablespoons coconut flour

1 teaspoon nut oil

STEPS FOR COOKING

1. In the mixing bowl mix up eggs with mashed bananas.

2. Then add ground cardamom, baking powder, coconut cream, coconut flour, and nut oil.

3. Stir the mixture with the help of the fork until smooth.

4. Then preheat the oven to 350F.

5. Pour the banana batter into the muffin molds and transfer them to the preheated oven.

6. Cook the muffins for 10 minutes.

7. Cool the cooked muffins and remove them from the molds.

STRAWBERRIES IN COCONUT CREAM

Time required:
15 minutes

Servings: 02

INGREDIENTS

1 cup strawberries

½ cup coconut cream

1 tablespoon coconut sugar

1 teaspoon vanilla extract

¼ teaspoon dried mint

STEPS FOR COOKING

1. In the mixing bowl mix up coconut cream, coconut sugar, vanilla extract, and dried mint.

2. Whisk the mixture until it is smooth and lightly fluffy.

3. Then chop the strawberries roughly and put them in the serving bowls.

4. Top the berries with a fluffy coconut cream mixture.

Chocolate Paleo Brownies

Time required:
35 minutes

Servings: 08

INGREDIENTS

1/4 cup cacao powder

1/2 tablespoon vanilla extract

¾ cup agave nectar

1 egg

8 ounces original almond butter

1/2 teaspoon baking soda

1 tablespoon extra virgin olive oil

1/4 teaspoon unrefined sea salt

1/2 cup dark chocolate chips

STEPS FOR COOKING

1. In a medium bowl, mix the almond butter, egg, nectar, and vanilla extract, then add the cacao powder, sea salt, and baking soda.

2. Fold in the chocolate chips. Pour the batter into a greased (extra virgin olive oil) "8 x 8" square baking dish. Bake at 325° for 30 min.

3. Make 8 brownies.

TOASTY SHORTBREAD COOKIES WITH PECANS

Time required:
25 minutes

Servings: 12

INGREDIENTS

1/2 cup pecans, chopped

2 1/2 tablespoons agave nectar

1 ¾ cups blanched almond flour

1/2 tablespoon vanilla extract

1/4 cup palm shortening, melted

1/8 teaspoon baking soda

Pinch of unrefined sea salt

STEPS FOR COOKING

1. In a large bowl, combine the almond flour, sea salt, baking soda, and pecans.

2. In another bowl combine the nectar, butter, and vanilla extract, then mix the wet ingredients into the dry ingredients.

3. Place the dough in the center of a piece of parchment paper.

4. Form the log into 1 3/4 inches in diameter. Freeze the log for one hour until firm.

5. Unwrap and cut into 1/4 inch slices, then place the slices on a parchment-lined baking sheet.

6. Bake at 350° for 10 min., cool, and serve. Makes 12 cookies.

CARROT FRIES

Time required:
20 minutes

Servings: 04

INGREDIENTS

2 carrots, peeled

1 tablespoon coconut oil

1 teaspoon dried dill

STEPS FOR COOKING

1. Cut the carrots on the French fries and sprinkle with dill.
2. Then put the coconut oil in the skillet and melt it.
3. Put the carrot fries in the skillet in one layer and roast for 3 minutes from each side on medium heat.
4. Then dry the cooked fries with the help of a paper towel.

ORANGE AND APRICOTS CAKE

Time required:
30 minutes

Servings: 08

INGREDIENTS

¾ cup stevia

2 cups almond flour

¼ cup olive oil

½ cup almond milk

1 teaspoon baking powder

2 eggs

½ teaspoon vanilla extract

Juice and zest of 2 oranges

2 cups apricots, chopped

STEPS FOR COOKING

1. In a bowl, blend the stevia plus the flour and the rest of the ingredients, whisk and pour into a cake pan lined with parchment paper.

2. Preheat oven to 375 degrees F and bake for 20 minutes.

3. Cool down, slice, and serve.

CHERRY CRISP

Time required:
25 minutes

Servings: 02

INGREDIENTS

1 cup cherry, pitted

1 teaspoon raw honey

1 tablespoon coconut flakes

½ teaspoon ground cinnamon

½ cup almond flour

1 tablespoon coconut shred

1 tablespoon coconut oil

STEPS FOR COOKING

1. Chop the cherries and mix them up with honey.
2. Then transfer the cherry mixture to the baking pan and flatten them.
3. After this, in the mixing bowl mix up coconut flakes, ground cinnamon, almond flour, coconut shred, and coconut oil.
4. Put the mixture over the cherries and gently stir.
5. Bake the cherry crisp for 15 minutes at 360F.

CREPE WITH FRESH FRUITS

Time required:
30 minutes

Servings: 06

INGREDIENTS

2 Tbsp. coconut flour

3 free-range eggs

1 tsp. raw honey

1/2 cup coconut milk

1 Tbsp. vanilla extract

Fresh fruit

Cinnamon

STEPS FOR COOKING

1. Mix flour, coconut milk, eggs, honey, and vanilla.

2. Heat a non-stick frypan greased with olive oil on med heat, then pour 1/4 cup of mixture into frypan; cooking till edges are light brown then flip to cook another side.

3. Repeat till batter is all gone; keeping crepes warm.

4. Fill each crepe with fresh fruit with some spilling out onto a plate for decoration.

5. Sprinkle lightly with cinnamon. You may also like to pour on some maple syrup.

Cocoa and Pears Cream

Time required:
10 minutes

Servings: 04

INGREDIENTS

2 cups heavy cream

1/3 cup stevia

¾ cup cocoa powder

6 ounces dark chocolate, chopped

Zest of 1 lemon

2 pears, chopped

STEPS FOR COOKING

1. In a blender, blend the cream plus the stevia and the rest of the ingredients.
2. Blend well.
3. Divide into cups and serve cold.

Fresh Fruit Salad

Time required:
30 minutes

Servings: 05

INGREDIENTS

Apples

Oranges

Grapes

Raspberries

Bananas

Kiwi Fruit

Watermelon

Cantaloupe

Blackberries

Blueberries

STEPS FOR COOKING

1. Simply place a combination of any of the above washed, chopped fresh fruits in a decorative serving bowl for a delicious dessert.

2. Sprinkle with blanched almonds for a treat.

3. Enjoy!

CPSIA information can be obtained
at www.ICGtesting.com
Printed in the USA
BVHW062320150621
609629BV00012B/1513